New Perspectives on
Essential Computer Concepts

Essential Computer Concepts

Photo Credits

Figure 1:   © PhotoDisc/Getty Images

Figure 3:   Courtesy of Acer America Inc.; Courtesy of Gateway Inc.; Courtesy of ViewSonic Corporation

Figure 4:   Courtesy of palmOne, Inc. palmOne, Zire, and Tungsten are among the trademarks owned by or exclusively licensed to palmOne, Inc.

Figure 5:   Courtesy of IBM Corporation

Figure 6:   Courtesy of NASA

Figure 7:   Courtesy of Microsoft Corporation

Figure 8:   Courtesy of Microsoft Corporation

Figure 10:   Courtesy of ViewSonic Corporation

Figure 11:   Courtesy of Lexmark International Inc.

Figure 20:   Courtesy of Seagate Technology

Figure 22:   Courtesy of Acer America Inc.

Objectives

In this tutorial, you will:
- Describe the components of a computer system
- Compare the types of computers
- Define a personal computer's hardware in terms of its functions: input, output, processing, and storage
- Examine data representation and the ASCII code
- Describe how peripheral devices are connected to a personal computer
- Identify the hardware and software that are used to establish a network connection
- Explain how Internet access, e-mail, and the World Wide Web affect the use of computers
- Discuss the types of system software and their functions
- Identify popular application software
- Describe how data is shared among different types of application software

Essential Computer Concepts

Case

Paik's Oriental Rug Gallery

Paik's Oriental Rug Gallery, located in the university town of Lake Thompson, specializes in the sale of new and used Oriental carpets. Paik's also performs beautiful renovations of damaged or old Oriental rugs. Thanks to his excellent customer service and professional reputation, owner Sang Kee Paik has broadened his customer base over the course of the last two years and is finding it hard to keep up with the paperwork. He recently hired you, a college graduate of the school of business, to assist him.

After several days on the job, you suggest to Mr. Paik that he would find it much easier to manage his inventory and payroll if he purchased several computers. He tells you he's considered that before, but hasn't had time to shop around. He asks you to research the features and prices of today's computers and recommend what he should purchase.

You go to the library to review computer trade magazines and examine the features of current models. Computers and their prices are constantly changing, but most of today's computers are well-suited to running a small business. You are sure you will be able to find computers that will meet Mr. Paik's needs. Figure 1 (on the next page) shows an advertisement for a computer you think might be appropriate for Mr. Paik's business.

Labs

Using a Mouse

Using a Keyboard

Peripheral Devices

Using Files

The Internet: World Wide Web

User Interfaces

Multimedia

Student Data Files

There are no student Data Files needed for this tutorial.

What Is a Computer?

Computers have become essential tools in almost every type of activity in virtually every type of business. A **computer** is defined as an electronic device that accepts input, processes data, stores data, and produces output. It is a versatile tool with the potential to perform many different tasks.

A **computer system** includes a computer, peripheral devices, and software. The physical components of a computer are referred to as **hardware**. The design and construction of a particular computer is referred to as its **architecture**, or **configuration**. The technical details about each component are called **specifications**. For example, a computer system might be *configured* to include a printer; a *specification* for that printer might be a print speed of eight pages per minute or the capacity to print in color. The computer itself takes care of the processing function, but it needs additional components, called **peripheral devices**, to accomplish its input, output, and storage functions. In this tutorial, you will learn more about the hardware that performs these basic computer functions.

Software refers to the intangible components of a computer system, particularly the **programs**, or lists of instructions, that the computer needs to perform a specific task. Software is the key to a computer's versatility. When your computer is using word processing software—for example, the Microsoft Word program—you can type memos, letters, and reports. When your computer is using accounting software, you can maintain information about what your customers owe you or display a graph showing the timing of customer payments.

The hardware and the software of a computer system work together to process data—the words, figures, sounds, and graphics that describe people, events, things, and ideas. Figure 2 illustrates how you and the computer system interact to complete a task. Suppose you want to use the computer to write a report. First you instruct the computer to use the word processing program. After activating the word processing program, you begin typing the text of your report. The data you type into the computer is called **input**. You use an **input device**, such as a keyboard or a mouse, to input data and issue commands. **Commands** are another type of input that instruct the computer on how to process the data. For example, in your report, you might want to center the title and double-space the text of the report. You issue the appropriate commands in the word processing program that will instruct the computer to modify the data you have input so the text is double-spaced and the title of the report is centered. Modifying data in this way is referred to as **processing**. In a computer, processing tasks occur on the **motherboard**, which is the main circuit board of the computer. The motherboard contains the **processing hardware**, the computer's major electronic components.

How a computer works ◄ **Figure 2**

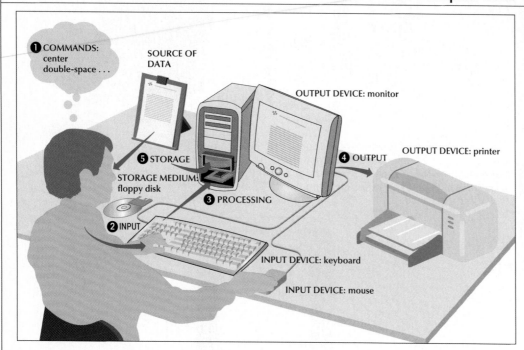

The result of the computer processing your input is referred to as **output**. Output can be in many different forms, for example reports, documents, graphs, sounds, and pictures. Computers produce output using **output devices**, such as a computer monitor or a printer. The output you create using a computer can be stored either inside the computer itself, or on an external storage device, such as a floppy disk. You will learn more about storage devices later in this tutorial.

Using a computer has several advantages. The first is the speed at which you can perform tasks. Second, the capability of storing the output and using it over and over again, in so many different ways, makes using a computer the most effective way to perform many personal and business tasks. Finally, an important advantage is sharing data and output with others. You make a note to find out whether Paik employees will need to share their data.

Types of Computers

There are many types of computers, which are classified by their size, speed, capabilities, and cost. Computers are categorized as personal computers, hand-held computers, mainframes, and supercomputers.

Personal computers, originally called **microcomputers**, are the computers typically used by a single user, for use in the home or office. Examples of personal computers are shown in Figure 3.

| Figure 3 | **Examples of personal computers** |

A desktop computer fits on a desk and runs on power from an electrical wall outlet. The monitor can be a flat panel monitor (like the one shown) or a CRT monitor, which takes up more space on the desk, but is less expensive.

A notebook computer is small and lightweight, giving it the advantage of portability. It can run on power supplied by an electrical outlet, or it can run on battery power.

A Tablet PC is a portable computer that has a screen on which the user can execute commands and write with a stylus. The computer recognizes the handwriting and integrates it into the program being used. On some models, the screen can be moved out of the way so that the user can access an attached keyboard; on other models, you can attach a keyboard if you wish.

A personal computer is used for general computing tasks such as word processing, working with photographs or graphics, e-mail, and Internet access. A personal computer is available as a **desktop computer**, which is designed to sit compactly on a desk; as a **notebook computer** (also referred to as a **laptop computer**), which is designed for portability; or as a **Tablet PC**, which is also designed for portability, but includes the capability of recognizing ordinary handwriting on the screen. Tablet PCs also include speech recognition software. Personal computers cost between $500 and $3000, but the average computer user spends $800 to $1300 when purchasing a personal computer. A notebook computer with similar capability is usually more expensive than a desktop computer, and Tablet PCs are more expensive than notebook computers.

Hand-held computers, also known as **PDAs** (Personal Digital Assistants), are small computers designed to fit in the palm of your hand, as shown in Figure 4. Hand-held computers are compact enough to fit in your pocket, and they run on batteries. Hand-held computers have more limited capabilities than personal computers, and are generally used to maintain an electronic appointment book, address book, calculator, and notepad, although high-end PDAs are all-in-one devices that can be used to send and receive e-mails and make phone calls. Hand-held computers cost between $100 and $700.

Example of a hand-held computer ◄ **Figure 4**

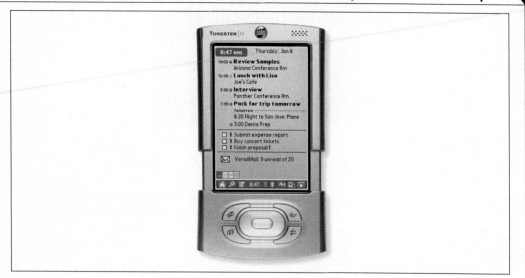

You assume that your recommendation to Mr. Paik will include personal computers because most daily tasks can be performed very efficiently using them. However, you wonder whether some employees might need the portability of notebook computers or Tablet PCs, and whether others might need a PDA. You add these notes to your list of questions to ask Mr. Paik.

Many small and large businesses use personal computers extensively. But some businesses, government agencies, and other institutions also use larger and faster types of computers such as mainframes and supercomputers. Usually, a company decides to purchase a mainframe computer when it must carry out the processing tasks for many users, especially when the users share large amounts of data. Each user inputs processing requests and views output through a terminal. A **terminal** has a keyboard for input and a monitor for output, but is not capable of processing data on its own.

Mainframe computers, like the one shown in Figure 5, are typically used to provide centralized storage, processing, and management for large amounts of data. The price of a mainframe computer varies widely, from several hundred thousand dollars to several million dollars.

The largest and fastest computers, called **supercomputers**, were first developed for high-volume computing tasks such as weather prediction. Supercomputers, like the one shown in Figure 6, are also being used by large corporations and government agencies when the tremendous volume of data would seriously delay processing on a mainframe computer. Although its cost can be tens of millions of dollars, a supercomputer's processing speed is so much faster than that of personal computers and mainframes that the investment can be worthwhile.

How would you classify the computer in the advertisement shown in Figure 1 at the beginning of the tutorial? If your answer is a desktop personal computer, you are correct. The computer in that ad fits on a desk and is not portable.

Based on what you have learned about the computing process and types of computers, you decide to recommend that Mr. Paik purchase some personal computers. When you look at the ad, however, you realize that there are several specifications that Mr. Paik may not understand. Your recommendation will have to explain what each listed component does, and why it is important. The remainder of this tutorial will focus on personal computer hardware and software in more detail, so you can learn what you need to know to make a better recommendation.

Computer Hardware

As you've already learned, computer hardware can be defined as the physical components of a computer. Now look at the hardware you might use in a typical personal computer system.

Input Devices

You input data and commands by using an input device such as a keyboard or a mouse. The computer can also receive input from a storage device. This section takes a closer look at the input devices you might use. Output and storage devices are covered in later sections.

The most frequently used input device is a **keyboard**. The top keyboard in Figure 7 is a standard 101-key keyboard. Newer keyboards, such as the bottom keyboard in Figure 7, are **ergonomic**, which means that they have been designed to fit the natural placement of your hands and should reduce the risk of repetitive-motion injuries. All keyboards consist of three major parts: the main keyboard, the keypads, and the function keys.

Using a Mouse

Using a Keyboard

Peripheral Devices

Keyboards ◄ **Figure 7**

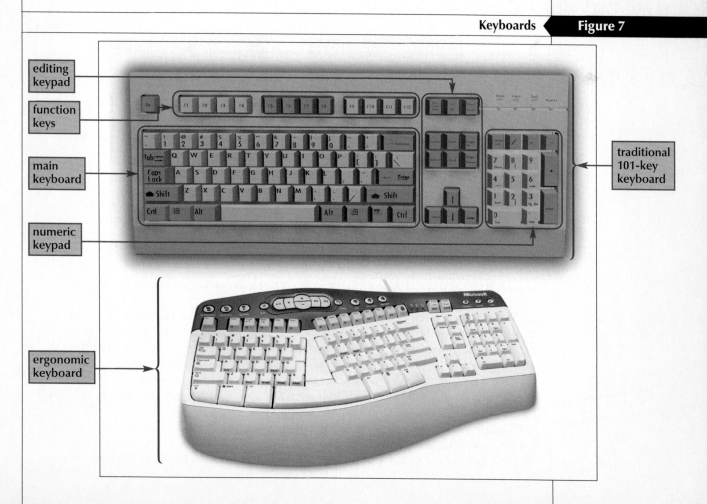

editing keypad

function keys

main keyboard

numeric keypad

ergonomic keyboard

traditional 101-key keyboard

All personal computers are equipped with a pointing device. The most popular is a **mouse**, such as the ones shown in Figure 8; notebook computers are usually equipped with one of the other options pictured in Figure 9.

Figure 8 ▶ **Personal computer pointing devices**

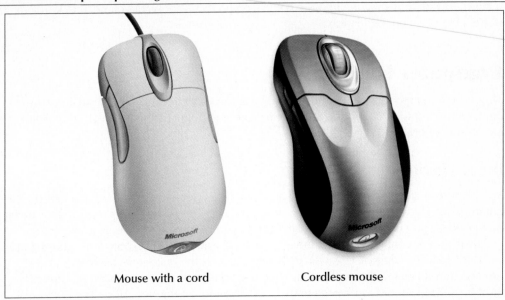

Mouse with a cord   Cordless mouse

Figure 9 ▶ **Notebook pointing devices**

Track point   Touch pad

A **track point** is a small eraser-like device embedded among the typing keys. To control the on-screen pointer, you push the track point up, left, right, or down. Buttons for clicking and double-clicking are located in front of the spacebar.

A **touch pad** is a touch-sensitive device. By dragging your finger over the surface, you control the on-screen pointer. Two buttons equivalent to mouse buttons are located in front of the touch pad.

The **pointing device** controls a **pointer**, a small arrow or other symbol, on the display screen. Using a pointing device is an important skill because most personal computers depend on such devices to select commands and manipulate text or graphics on the screen. People with physical impairments or disabilities can also use pointing devices because of recent advances in making computers accessible to everyone. For example, people who do not have the use of their arms can use adaptive pointing devices to control the pointer with foot, head, or eye movements.

Computers used for presentations often feature remote input devices, sometimes called **wireless pointers**, that work like the remote control used for a TV, VCR, or DVD. The remote input device allows you to control the pointer from the back of the auditorium.

Now that you have read about input devices, refer back to the computer advertisement shown in Figure 1 at the beginning of the tutorial. Can you list the input devices included with the advertised system? A mouse and a keyboard are considered essential peripheral devices, so advertisements do not always list them. Unless the ad specifies some other input device, such as a track ball, you can safely assume the computer comes equipped with a traditional keyboard and mouse.

Output Devices

As stated earlier, output is the result of processing data; output devices show you those results. The most commonly used output devices are monitors and printers. A **monitor** is the device that displays the output from a computer, as shown in Figure 10. The monitor on the left is a **CRT (cathode ray tube) monitor**, which uses gun-like devices that direct beams of electrons toward the screen to activate dots of color to form the image you see on the screen. The monitor on the right is a **flat panel monitor**. Most flat panel monitors use **LCD (liquid crystal display)** technology, which creates the image you see on the screen by manipulating light within a layer of liquid crystal. This is the same technology used in digital watches or the time display on a microwave oven. Flat panel display monitors take up very little room on the desktop, are lightweight, and are very easy to read, but are much more expensive than CRT monitors. However, many graphic artists prefer CRT technology because it displays uniform color from any viewing angle.

Monitor types ◄ **Figure 10**

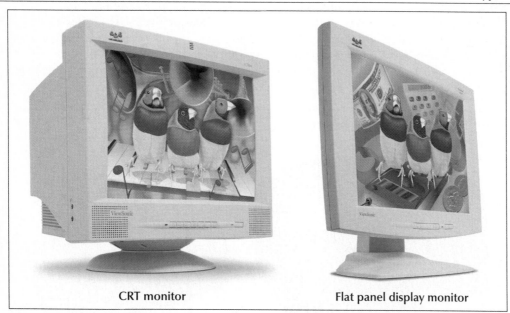

CRT monitor   Flat panel display monitor

Factors that influence the quality of a monitor are screen size, resolution, and dot pitch. **Screen size** is the diagonal measurement in inches from one corner of the screen to the other. Measurements for today's desktop monitors range from 15" to 23". The monitors on notebook computers range from 12" to 17". The first personal computer monitors and many terminals still in use today are character-based. A **character-based display** divides the screen into a grid of rectangles, one for each typed character. A monitor that is capable of displaying graphics, called a **graphics display**, divides the screen into a matrix of small dots called **pixels**. **Resolution** is the maximum number of pixels the monitor can display. Standard resolutions are 640 × 480, 800 × 600, 1,024 × 768, 1,280 × 1,024, and 1,600 × 1,200. The resolution you use depends on your monitor size. If your screen is small, 1,600 × 1,200 resolution will make the objects on the screen too small to see clearly. Resolution is easy to adjust on most monitors. **Dot pitch** measures the distance between pixels, so a smaller dot pitch means a sharper image. A .28 or .26 dot pitch (dp) is typical for today's monitors.

A computer display system consists of a monitor and a **graphics card**, also called a **video display adapter** or **video card**. A **card** is a rigid piece of insulating material with circuits on it. The circuits control the functions of the card. The graphics card is installed inside the computer on the motherboard, and controls the signals the computer sends to the monitor. If you plan to display a lot of images on the monitor, you may also need a **graphics accelerator card** to speed up the computer's ability to display them. When purchasing a monitor, you must be sure that it comes with a video card that is compatible with your computer.

Refer back to the computer ad in Figure 1. Does this personal computer include a monitor and video card? The correct answer is yes, both are included. What is the type, size, and resolution of the monitor? The monitor is a 15" 1,024 × 768 flat panel monitor.

A **printer** produces a paper copy of the text or graphics processed by the computer. A printed copy of computer output is called **hard copy**, because it is more tangible than the electronic or magnetic copies found on a disk, in the computer memory, or on the monitor. There are three popular categories of printers, and each has special capabilities.

The most popular printers for business use are **laser printers**, like the one shown on the left in Figure 11, because they use the same technology as a photocopier. A temporary laser image is transferred onto paper with a powdery substance called **toner**. This produces high-quality output quickly and efficiently. The speed of laser printers is measured in **pages per minute (ppm)**. Color laser printers use several toner cartridges to apply color to the page. Non-color laser printers are less expensive than color laser printers.

A less expensive alternative to the laser printer is to use a color **inkjet printer** such as the one shown on the right in Figure 11. These printers spray ink onto paper. The quality of the inkjet output is almost comparable to a laser printer's output. Inkjet printers, with and without color capabilities, are very popular printers for home use. The speed of inkjet printers is also measured in pages per minute.

Figure 11	Types of printers

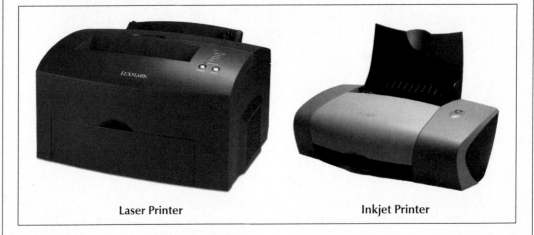

Laser Printer   Inkjet Printer

Another type of printer is the dot matrix printer, the oldest printing technology currently found on the computer market. Dot matrix printers transfer ink to the paper by striking a ribbon with pins. Using more pins controls the quality of the print, so a 24-pin dot matrix printer produces better quality print than a 9-pin. Dot matrix printers are most often used when a large number of pages need to be printed fairly quickly or when a business needs to print on multi-page continuous forms. The speed of dot matrix printers is measured in characters per second (cps). Some examples of their usefulness are the printing of grade reports, bank statements, or payroll checks.

You notice that the computer ad in Figure 1 does not include a printer, so you make a note to ask Mr. Paik if your recommendation should include one. If so, you decide to recommend a color laser printer to print correspondence, advertisements, and brochures.

Multimedia devices are another category of peripheral devices. **Multimedia** refers to an integrated collection of computer-based media including text, graphics, sound, animation, and video. Most personal computers come equipped with a sound card and speakers that can play digital sounds. The sound card converts sounds so that they can be broadcast through speakers.

The computer advertised in Figure 1 includes a sound card and speakers that are built into the monitor. These are also output devices that you need to mention in your recommendation. Mr. Paik will need these output devices for a variety of activities, such as participating in teleconferences on product availability attended by suppliers in widespread locations, or recording announcements that employees can play back at their convenience. Later in this tutorial, you will learn how business users are sharing a variety of data resources, including digital sound.

Using Files

Processing Hardware

The most important computer function is processing data. Before you can understand this function and the hardware that executes it, you first need to learn how the computer represents and stores data.

Data Representation

The characters used in human language are meaningless to a computer because it is an electronic device. Like a light bulb, the computer must interpret every signal as either "on" or "off." To do so, a computer represents data as distinct or separate numbers. Specifically, it represents "on" with a 1 and "off" with a 0. These numbers are referred to as **binary digits**, or **bits**.

A series of eight bits is called a **byte**. As Figure 12 shows, the byte that represents the integer value 0 is 00000000, with all eight bits "off" or set to 0. The byte that represents the integer value 1 is 00000001, and the byte that represents 255 is 11111111.

Binary representation of numbers ◄ **Figure 12**

Number	Binary Representation
0	00000000
1	00000001
2	00000010
3	00000011
4	00000100
5	00000101
6	00000110
7	00000111
8	00001000
⋮	⋮
253	11111101
254	11111110
255	11111111

Personal computers commonly use the **ASCII** code to represent character data. ASCII (pronounced "ASK-ee") stands for **American Standard Code for Information Interchange**. The ASCII system translates the decimal numbers 0 through 255 into binary data. Each ASCII code represents a letter or character on the keyboard; for example, the ASCII code 65 represents the character *A*, and the ASCII code 97 represents *a*. Computers translate ASCII code into binary data so that they can process it. Figure 13 shows sample ASCII code.

Figure 13 | Sample ASCII code representing letters and symbols

Character	ASCII code	Binary Number
(space)	32	00100000
$	36	00100100
A	65	01000001
B	66	01000010
a	97	01100001
b	98	01100010

As a computer user, you don't have to know the binary representations of numbers, characters, and instructions, because the computer handles all the necessary conversions internally. However, because the amount of memory in a computer and its storage capacity are expressed in bytes, you should be aware of how data is represented. **Storage**, or **memory capacity**, is the amount of data, or number of characters, that the device can handle at any given time. A **kilobyte** (KB or simply K) is 1,024 bytes, or approximately one thousand bytes. A **megabyte** (MB) is 1,048,576 bytes, or about one million bytes. A **gigabyte** (GB) is 1,073,741,824 bytes, or about one billion bytes. You will see the symbols KB, MB, and GB refer to both processing and storage capacity.

The Microprocessor

The two most important components of personal computer hardware are the **microprocessor**, a silicon chip designed to manipulate data, and the **memory**, which stores instructions and data. The type of microprocessor and the memory capacity are two factors that directly affect the price and performance of a computer.

The microprocessor, such as the one shown in Figure 14, is an integrated circuit (an electronic component called a **chip**) which is located on the motherboard inside the computer. The terms **processor** and **central processing unit** (CPU) also refer to this device, which is responsible for executing instructions to process data.

Figure 14 | An Intel Pentium 4 microprocessor

The speed of a microprocessor is determined by its clock speed, word size, and cache size. Think of the **clock speed** as the pulse of the processor. It is measured in millions of cycles per second, or **megahertz** (MHz), or **gigahertz** (GHz), a billion cycles per second. **Word size** refers to the number of bits that are processed at one time. A computer with a large word size can process faster than a computer with a small word size. The earliest personal computers had an 8-bit word size, but now a 64-bit word size is common. **Cache**, sometimes called **RAM cache** or **cache memory**, is special high-speed memory reserved for the microprocessor's use. It speeds up the processing function by accessing data the computer anticipates you will request soon, while you are still working on something else.

Take another look at the computer advertised in Figure 1. What is the type and speed of its microprocessor? Your answer should be that it has a Pentium 4 microprocessor that can operate at 2.66 GHz and has 512 K cache.

Memory

Computer **memory** is a set of storage locations on the motherboard. Your computer has four types of memory: random access memory, virtual memory, read-only memory, and complementary metal oxide semiconductor (CMOS) memory.

Random access memory (RAM) is active during the processing function. It consists of electronic circuits on the motherboard that temporarily hold programs and data while the computer is on. RAM is **volatile**, which means that it is constantly changing as long as the computer is on and is cleared when the computer is turned off. The microprocessor uses RAM to store and retrieve instructions and data as they are needed. For example, if you are writing a paper, the word processing program that you are using is temporarily copied into RAM so the microprocessor can quickly access the instructions that you will need as you type and format your paper. As you type, the characters are also stored in RAM, along with the many fonts, special characters, graphics, and other objects that you might use to enhance the paper. How much you can include in your paper depends on the RAM capacity of the computer you are using. Most personal computers on the market today use **SDRAM** (synchronous dynamic RAM) or **RDRAM** (Rambus dynamic RAM). SDRAM is plenty fast for the average computer user and inexpensive. RDRAM was originally designed for use in computer game systems and is more expensive than SDRAM. When paired with a microprocessor of 1 GHz or faster, RDRAM can improve a computer system's overall performance.

Look at the computer ad in Figure 1. Notice that this computer has 512 MB of SDRAM. In other words, it has the capacity to temporarily store over 512 million characters at any one time. Although your paper might not be that long, the computer uses a lot of that available memory for programs and other data it needs to process your paper. The notation "expandable to 2 GB (2048 MB)" tells you that you can add more RAM to this computer. Expandability is an important feature of any computer; you need to be able to change your computer's capability as your needs change.

When the programs running on a computer use all the available RAM, the software uses space on the computer's storage devices to simulate RAM. This extra memory is called **virtual memory**. Figure 15 explains how it works. The disadvantage of using virtual memory is that it is much slower than RAM, so expanding the RAM capacity of a computer will improve its performance.

Figure 15   **How virtual memory works**

1. Your computer is running a word processing program that takes up most of the program area in RAM, but you want to run a spreadsheet program at the same time.

2. The operating system moves the least-used segment of the word processing program into virtual memory on disk.

3. The spreadsheet program can now be loaded into the RAM vacated by the least-used segment of the word processing program.

4. If the least-used segment of the word processing program is later needed, it is copied from virtual memory back into RAM. To make room, some other infrequently used segment of a program will need to be transferred into virtual memory.

Read-only memory (ROM) is another set of electronic circuits on the motherboard inside the computer. Although you can expand your RAM capacity, you cannot add to ROM capacity. In fact, the manufacturer of the computer permanently installs ROM. It is the permanent storage location for a set of instructions that the computer uses when you turn it on. Because ROM never changes and it remains intact when the computer is turned off, it is called **nonvolatile**.

The events that occur between the moment you turn on the computer and the moment you can actually begin to use the computer are called the **boot process**, as shown in Figure 16, and the act of turning on the computer is sometimes called **booting up**. When the computer is off, RAM is empty. When the computer is turned on, the set of instructions in ROM checks all the computer system's components to make sure they are working, and activates the essential software that controls the processing function.

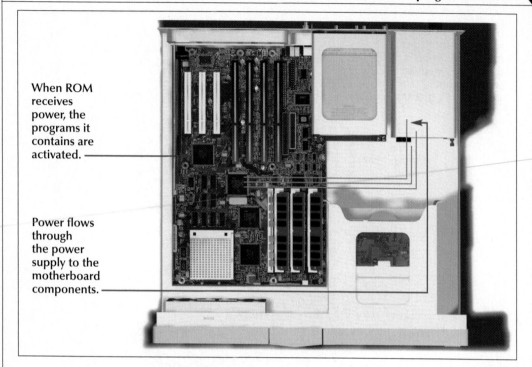

When ROM receives power, the programs it contains are activated. ——

Power flows through the power supply to the motherboard components. ——

Complementary metal oxide semiconductor (CMOS) memory (pronounced "SEE-Moss") is another chip that is installed on the motherboard. It is also activated during the boot process and contains information about where the essential software is stored. A small rechargeable battery powers CMOS so its contents will be saved between computer uses. Unlike ROM, which cannot be changed, CMOS must be changed every time you add or remove hardware to your computer system. Thus, CMOS is often referred to as semipermanent memory, ROM as permanent memory, and RAM as temporary memory.

Storage Devices and Media

Because RAM retains data only while the power is on, your computer must have a more permanent storage option. As Figure 17 shows, a storage device receives data from RAM and writes it on a storage medium, such as a disk. Later the data can be read and sent back to RAM to use again.

Figure 17	Storage devices and RAM

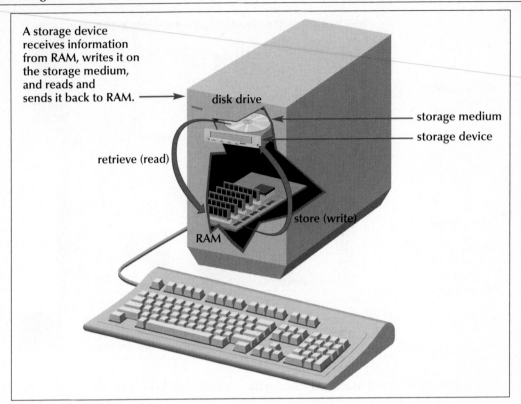

A storage device receives information from RAM, writes it on the storage medium, and reads and sends it back to RAM.

disk drive

storage medium

storage device

retrieve (read)

store (write)

RAM

Before you can understand the hardware that stores data, you need to know how data is stored. All data and programs are stored as files. A computer **file** is a named collection of related bits that exists on a storage medium. There are two categories of files: executable files and data files. An **executable file** contains the instructions that tell a computer how to perform a specific task. The files that are used during the boot process, for instance, are executable. Users create **data files**, usually with software. For instance, a paper that you write with a word processing program is data, and must be saved as a data file if you want to use it again.

The storage devices where computer files are kept can be categorized by the method they use to store files. **Magnetic storage devices** use oxide-coated plastic storage media called **mylar**. Figure 18 illustrates the process of storing data on magnetic media.

Storing data on magnetic media ◄ **Figure 18**

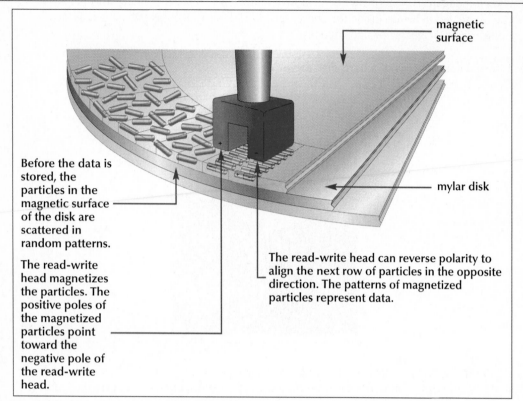

magnetic
surface

mylar disk

Before the data is stored, the particles in the magnetic surface of the disk are scattered in random patterns.

The read-write head magnetizes the particles. The positive poles of the magnetized particles point toward the negative pole of the read-write head.

The read-write head can reverse polarity to align the next row of particles in the opposite direction. The patterns of magnetized particles represent data.

The most common magnetic storage devices are floppy disk drives, hard disk drives, and tape drives. **Floppy disks**, sometimes called **diskettes**, are flat circles of iron oxide-coated plastic enclosed in a hard plastic case (see Figure 19). Floppy disks are sometimes called 3½" disks because of the size of the hard plastic case. Floppy disks have the capacity to store 1.44 MB, or 1,440,000 bytes, of data. Although some computers are now manufactured without a floppy disk drive, floppy disks are still very common. The computer shown in the advertisement in Figure 1 has a floppy disk drive that accepts 3½" floppy disks with 1.44 MB capacity.

3½" disk ◄ **Figure 19**

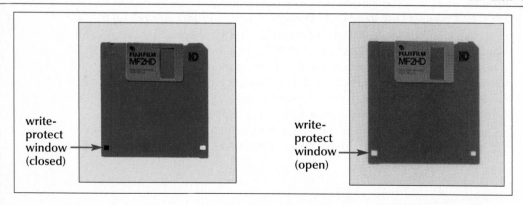

write-protect window (closed)

write-protect window (open)

Write protection prevents additional files from being stored on the disk and any file from being erased from the disk. To write protect a 3½" floppy disk, you open the write-protect window, as shown in Figure 19.

The other most common magnetic storage device is a **hard disk drive**, such as the one shown in Figure 20. This drive contains several iron oxide-covered metal platters that are usually sealed in a case inside the computer. Hard disk storage has two advantages over floppy disk storage: speed and capacity.

Figure 20 ⟩ **Internal components of a hard disk drive**

The speed of a disk drive is measured by its **access time**, the time required to read or write one record of data. Access time is measured in **milliseconds** (ms), one-thousandths of a second. The hard disk drive included in Figure 1, for instance, has 6 ms access time. Its capacity is 80 GB. Although this seems like a very high number, a Windows-based computer fully loaded with typical software can use up to 1 GB, and the addition of data and multimedia files can add up quickly.

Another magnetic storage device is a **tape drive**, which provides inexpensive archival storage for large quantities of data. Tape storage is much too slow to be used for day-to-day computer tasks; therefore, tapes are used to make backup copies of data stored on hard disks. If a hard disk fails, data from the backup tape can be reloaded on a new hard disk with minimal interruption of operations. Large corporations use tape drives for backup, but smaller companies and home computer systems rely on other storage methods.

Optical storage devices use laser technology to read and write data on silver platters. The first standard optical storage device on personal computers was the **CD-ROM** drive, which stands for **Compact Disk Read Only Memory**. One CD-ROM can store up to 700 MB, equivalent to more than 450 floppy disks. Today's personal computers are also equipped with **DVD**, or **Digital Video Disk**, drives. DVDs, though the same size as CD-ROMs, can store up to 4.7 GB of data, depending on whether data is stored on one or two sides of the disk, and how many layers of data each side contains. This is a little less than seven times the capacity of a CD. A DVD has more than enough storage capacity for an entire feature-length film—up to 9 hours of video or 30 hours of CD-ROM-quality audio.

Optical storage technology records data as a trail of tiny pits in the disk surface. The data that these pits represent can then be "read" with a beam of laser light. Figure 21 shows how data is stored on optical media.

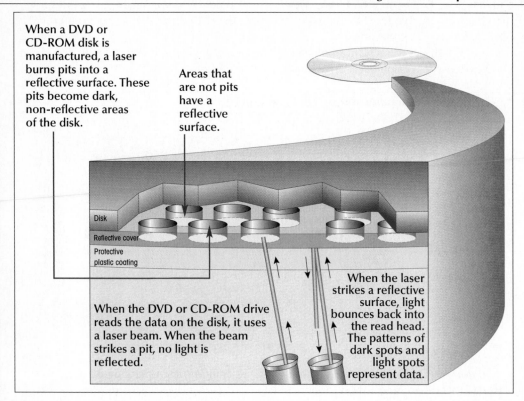

When a DVD or CD-ROM disk is manufactured, a laser burns pits into a reflective surface. These pits become dark, non-reflective areas of the disk.

Areas that are not pits have a reflective surface.

Disk

Reflective cover

Protective plastic coating

When the DVD or CD-ROM drive reads the data on the disk, it uses a laser beam. When the beam strikes a pit, no light is reflected.

When the laser strikes a reflective surface, light bounces back into the read head. The patterns of dark spots and light spots represent data.

The most common uses of CD-ROMs or DVDs are for software distribution and storing large files that typically include graphics, animation, and video. Optical storage media are very durable. Unlike magnetic media, such as floppy and hard disks, CD and DVD platters are not susceptible to humidity, dust, fingerprints, or magnets. They are not indestructable, however. Take care not to scratch the disk surface or expose the disk to high temperatures.

CD-ROMs are for "read-only" access, meaning you can read data stored on them, but you cannot use them to record or store your own data. In order to record data on a CD, you need a **CD-R** (compact disc recordable) drive and a CD-R disk. Instead of storing data in pits made on the surface of the disk, as with a CD-ROM drive, the drive is designed so that a laser changes the reflectivity of a dye layer on a blank CD-R disk, creating dark spots on the disk's surface that represent the data. Once the data is recorded, you cannot erase or modify it, but you can append new data to the data currently stored on the CD-R disk. A **CD-RW** (compact disk rewritable) drive is designed so that you can write data on a special CD-RW disk and continually access and modify that data. CD-R disks can be read by a standard CD-ROM drive or a DVD drive; CD-RW disks can be read only by CD-RW drives or CD-ROM drives labeled "multi-read."

Both CD-Rs and CD-RWs are useful for storing large amounts of data, or for transferring large files from one computer to another. The original CD-ROM drive had a relatively slow access time: 600 ms. As the technology has improved, that access time has decreased to less than 200 ms. A lower number means faster access. Also consider the drive's data transfer rate, measured in kilobits per second (**Kbps**), to classify it as 1X (the original), 2X (twice the original), 3X, and so on.

Recordable DVD drives are becoming more common. As with CDs, you can buy a DVD to which you can record only once, or a rewritable DVD to which you can record and then re-record data. Recordable and rewriteable DVDs come in several formats; for example, recordable DVDs are available as DVD-R and DVD+R. Make sure you know which type of DVD your DVD drive uses. The computer shown in Figure 1 includes a 4x recordable/rewritable DVD drive. It supports both the -RW and +RW formats, and it can read and record CDs as well.

Figure 22 shows the typical storage configuration of a personal computer. It includes a DVD±RW drive, a floppy disk drive, and a hard drive.

Figure 22 ▷ **Typical personal computer storage configuration**

DVD±RW drive

3½" disk drive

indicator light for hard drive

You decide that your recommendation to Mr. Paik should include computers with at least CD-RW drives, and some computers with DVD±RW drives. As computers are used, the storage devices fill up quickly with software and data, so it's a good idea to purchase as much storage capacity as your budget allows. Even though floppy disks are becoming less popular as recordable CD and DVD drives drop in price, they are still frequently used, so you will include them, too. You also decide to recommend at least 80 GB hard drives and perhaps 120 GB hard drives for some of the machines. You will also recommend at least 512 MB of RAM for each machine.

Data Communications

The transmission of text, numeric, voice, or video data from one computer to another is called **data communications**. This broad-based definition encompasses many critical business activities, from sending a letter to the printer upstairs to sending an **e-mail (electronic mail)** message to the company offices around the globe.

The four essential components of data communications are a sender, a receiver, a channel, and a protocol. The computer that originates the message is the **sender**. The message is sent over some type of **channel**, such as telephone or coaxial cable, a microwave signal, or optical fibers. The computer at the message's destination is called the **receiver**. The rules that establish an orderly transfer of data between the sender and the receiver are called **protocols**. Communication software and hardware establish these protocols at the beginning of the transmission, and both computers follow them strictly to guarantee an accurate transfer of data.

Data Bus

As noted earlier, peripherals are devices that can be added to a computer system to enhance its usefulness. Starting at the microprocessor, and passing through a continuous channel, the data travels out to the appropriate device. From an input device back to the microprocessor, the path is reversed. This communication between the microprocessor, RAM, and the peripherals is called the **data bus**.

An external peripheral device must have a corresponding **port** and **cable** that connect it to the back of the computer. Inside the computer, each port connects to a **controller card**, sometimes called an **expansion** or **interface card**. These cards, which provide an electrical connection to a variety of peripheral devices, plug into electrical connectors on the motherboard called **slots** or **expansion slots**. Figure 23 shows the data path that connects a printer to a computer. An internal peripheral device such as a hard disk drive may plug directly into the motherboard, or it may have an attached controller card. The transmission protocol is handled by a **device driver**, or simply **driver**, which is a computer program that can establish communication because it contains information about the characteristics of your computer and of the device.

Components for connecting a printer to a computer ◀ **Figure 23**

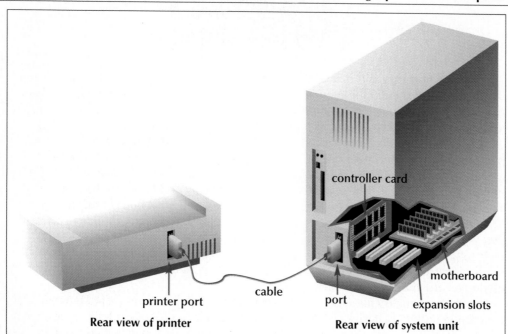

Personal computers can have several types of ports, including USB, parallel, serial, SCSI, and MIDI. Figure 24 diagrams how the ports on a desktop personal computer might appear.

Figure 24 **Computer expansion ports**

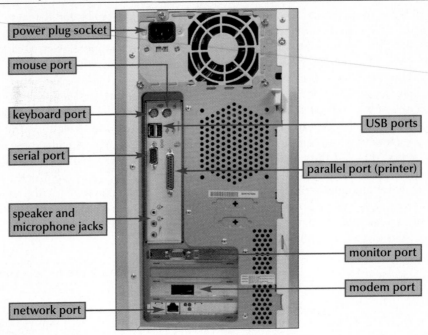

power plug socket

mouse port

keyboard port

serial port

speaker and microphone jacks

network port

USB ports

parallel port (printer)

monitor port

modem port

A **parallel port** transmits data eight bits at a time. Parallel transmissions are relatively fast, but increase the risk for interference, so they are typically used to connect a printer that is near the computer. A **serial port** transmits data one bit at a time. Typically, a mouse, keyboard, and modem are connected with serial interfaces.

SCSI (pronounced "scuzzy") stands for **small computer system interface**. One SCSI port provides an interface for one or more peripheral devices. The first is connected directly to the computer through the port, and the second device is plugged into a similar port on the first device. SCSI connections can allow many devices to use the same port. They are particularly popular on Macintosh computers and notebook computers.

Figure 24 shows some other ports for telephone cables to connect a modem, a video port to connect a monitor, and a network port. The interface to a sound card usually includes jacks for speakers and a microphone, which are designed to work with a **MIDI (musical instrument digital interface) card**, which is pronounced "middy." MIDI cards are used to record and play back musical data.

Notebook computers may also include a **Personal Computer Memory Card International Association (PCMCIA) device**. PCMCIA devices are credit-card-sized cards that plug directly into the PCMCIA slot and can contain additional memory, a modem, or a hard disk drive.

Another type of port found in computers is a **USB (Universal Serial Bus) port**. USB is a high-speed technology that facilitates the connection of external devices, such as joysticks, scanners, keyboards, video conferencing cameras, speakers, modems, and printers, to a computer. The device you install must have a **USB connector**, a small rectangular plug. You simply plug the USB connector into the USB port, and the computer recognizes the device and allows you to use it immediately. USB-compatible computers work more like stereo systems, in that you don't have to completely disassemble the unit to add a component. Any USB device can use any USB port, interchangeably and in any order. You can "daisy chain" up to 127 devices, plugging one device into another, or you can connect multiple devices to a single inexpensive hub. Data is transferred through a USB port 10 times faster than through a serial port, for example. For many USB devices, power is supplied via the port, so there is no need for extra power cables. Older computers can have numerous connectors—a keyboard connector, a mouse port, a parallel port, a joystick port, two audio ports, and two serial ports. USB computers replace this proliferation of ports with one standardized plug and port combination.

Look at the computer advertised in Figure 1. Does this computer include any of the ports illustrated in Figure 24? It mentions PS/2, USB, and parallel ports. Ports for a monitor, mouse, and keyboard are also included, because the advertisement lists those devices.

Networks

One of the most important types of data communications in the business world is a network connection. A **network** connects one computer to other computers and peripheral devices, enabling you to share data and resources with your coworkers. There are a variety of network configurations, too many to discuss thoroughly here. However, any type of network has some basic characteristics and requirements that you should know.

In a **local area network** (LAN), computers and peripheral devices are located relatively close to each other, generally in the same building. If you are using such a network, it is useful to know three things: the location of the data, the type of network card in your computer, and the communications software that manages protocols and network functions.

Some networks have one or more computers, called **servers**, that act as the central storage location for programs and provide mass storage for most of the data used on the network. A network with a server and computers dependent on the server is called a **client/server network**. The dependent computers are the **clients**. These networks are dependent on the server because it contains most of the data and software. When a network does not have a server, all the computers essentially are equal, and programs and data are distributed among them. This is called a **peer-to-peer network**.

Each computer that is part of the network must have a **network interface card (NIC)** installed. This card creates a communications channel between the computer and the network. A cable is used to connect the NIC port to the network. **Wi-Fi** (short for wireless fidelity) refers to a high-frequency **wireless local area network (WLAN)**. Wi-Fi is used to connect computers in a network by transmitting data through the air from an alternative to a wired LAN. Wi-Fi can be especially useful in buildings with older wiring. **Network software** is also essential, establishing the communications protocols that will be observed on the network and controlling the "traffic flow" as data travels throughout the network.

A personal computer that is not connected to a network is called a **standalone computer**. When it is connected to the network, it becomes a **workstation**. You have already learned that a terminal has a keyboard and monitor used for input and output, but it is not capable of processing on its own. A terminal is connected to a network that uses mainframes as servers. Any device connected to the network is called a **node**. Figure 25 illustrates a typical network configuration.

Network nodes include workstations, printers, and servers ◄ **Figure 25**

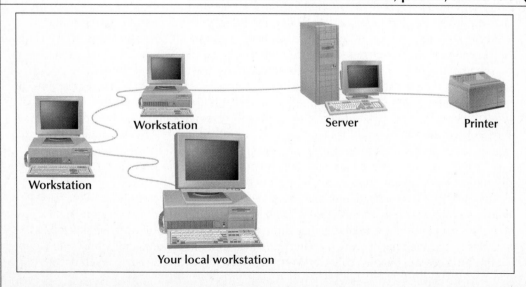

Workstation

Workstation

Your local workstation

Server

Printer

Look at the computer ad in Figure 1. Is this computer networked? Can it be networked? Why or why not? Your answer should be that the computer is not currently part of a network but does include an integrated network adapter card. With the appropriate network software, this computer can be connected to a network.

Telecommunications

Telecommunications means communicating over a comparatively long distance using a phone line. When it is not possible to connect users on one network, then telecommunications allows you to send and receive data over the telephone lines. To make this connection, you must use a communications device called a **modem**. A modem, which stands for *modulator-demo*dulator, is a device that connects your computer to a standard telephone jack. The modem converts the **digital**, or stop-start, **signals** your computer outputs into **analog**, or continuous wave, **signals** (sound waves) that can traverse ordinary phone lines. Figure 26 shows the telecommunications process, in which a modem converts digital signals to analog signals at the sending site (modulates) and a second modem converts the analog signals back into digital signals at the receiving site (demodulates).

| Figure 26 | Using modems to send and receive a memo |

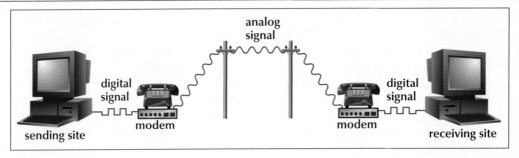

Most computers today come with a built-in 56K modem. The number 56 represents the modem's capability to send and receive about 56,000 **bits per second (bps)**. Actual speed may be reduced by factors such as distance, technical interference, and other issues. This speed is adequate for Paik employees to connect to suppliers at other locations around the world.

**The Internet:
World Wide
Web**

The Internet

The Internet was originally developed for the government to connect researchers around the world who needed to share data. Today, the **Internet** is the largest network in the world, connecting millions of people. It has become an invaluable communications channel for individuals, businesses, and governments around the world.

The first Internet experience most people have is to use **electronic mail**, more commonly called **e-mail**. This is the capability to send a message from one user's computer to another user's computer where it is stored until the receiver opens it. The vast network of networks that make up the Internet pass the message along through electronic links called **gateways**. E-mail has become such an integral part of business that you know you must recommend it to Mr. Paik. Your recommendation will list its advantages: speed and ease of communication with vendors and customers, lower postage costs, lower long-distance charges, and increased worker productivity.

Another benefit of using the Internet is the emergence of the **World Wide Web**, sometimes referred to simply as the **Web**. The Web is a huge database of information that is stored on network servers in places that allow public access. The information is stored as text files called **Web pages**, which can include text, graphics, sound, animation, and video. A collection of Web pages is called a **Web site**. Figure 27 shows a sample Web page.

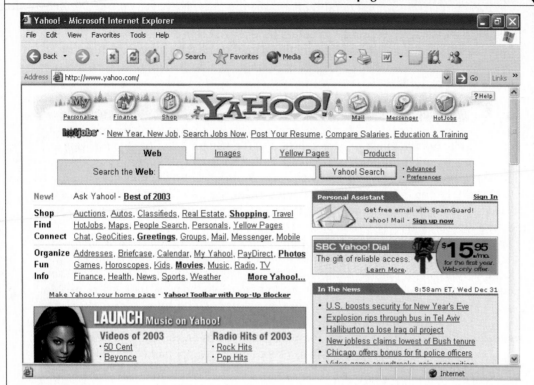

The evolution of multimedia and Internet technologies has made the World Wide Web the perfect communications tool for marketing business services and products. Hyperlinks are the primary resource for making the Web possible. A **hyperlink**, or **link**, is a place on a Web page that is programmed to connect to a particular file on the same network server, or even on a network server on the other side of the globe. The communications software that helps you navigate the World Wide Web is called **Web browsing software**, or a **Web browser**. You decide to include the benefits of Internet and World Wide Web access in your recommendation to Mr. Paik. Specifically, you plan to convince him that he could sell carpets and advertise his carpet renovation services through the Web.

Computer Software

Just as a tape player or DVD player is worthless without tapes or DVDs, computer hardware is useless without software. **Software** is defined as the instructions and associated data that direct the computer to accomplish a task. Sometimes the term *software* refers to a single program, but often the term refers to a collection of programs and data that are packaged together. A **software package** contains disks or a CD-ROM and reference manual. The CD-ROM contains one or more programs and possibly some data. For example, the Microsoft Office 2003 software includes programs that help you draw graphics, create documents, and make calculations. The software includes some data, such as a thesaurus of words and their synonyms.

Software can be divided into two major categories: system software and application software. **System software** helps the computer carry out its basic operating tasks. **Application software** helps the user carry out a variety of tasks.

User Interfaces

System Software

System software manages the fundamental operations of your computer, such as loading programs and data into memory, executing programs, saving data to disks, displaying information on the monitor, and transmitting data through a port to a peripheral device. There are four types of system software: operating systems, utilities, device drivers, and programming languages.

An **operating system** controls basic input and output, allocates system resources, manages storage space, maintains security, and detects equipment failure. You have already learned the importance of data communications, both from a standalone computer and from a workstation to other users on a network. The flow of data from the microprocessor to memory to peripherals and back again is called basic **I/O**, or **i**nput/**o**utput. The operating system controls this flow of data just as an air-traffic controller manages airport traffic.

A system resource is any part of the computer system, including memory, storage devices, and the microprocessor, that can be used by a computer program. The operating system allocates system resources so programs run properly. Most of today's computers are capable of **multitasking**—opening and running more than one program at a time—because the operating system is allocating memory and processing time to make multitasking possible. An example of multitasking is producing a document in your word processing program while you check a resource on the Internet. Both the word processing program and the Web browsing program are allowed to use parts of the computer's resources, so you can look at the resource periodically while you are writing about it in your paper. The operating system is also responsible for managing the files on your storage devices. Not only does it open and save files, but it also keeps track of every part of every file for you and lets you know if any part is missing. This activity is like a filing clerk who puts files away when they are not being used, and gets them for you when you need them again.

While you are working on the computer, the operating system is constantly guarding against equipment failure. Each electronic circuit is checked periodically, and the moment a problem is detected, the user is notified with a warning message on the screen.

The operating system's responsibility to maintain security may include requiring a username and password or checking the computer for virus infection. Unscrupulous programmers deliberately construct harmful programs, called **viruses**, which instruct your computer to perform destructive activities, such as erasing a disk drive. Some viruses are more annoying than destructive, but some can be harmful, erasing data or causing your hard disk to require reformatting. Computer users should protect themselves from viruses by using virus protection software. **Virus protection software** searches executable files for the sequences of characters that may cause harm and disinfects the files by erasing or disabling those commands. The computer advertised in Figure 1 comes with virus protection software preinstalled, and with the operating system Windows XP Professional.

Microsoft Windows, used on many personal computers, and the MAC OS, used exclusively on Macintosh computers, are referred to as **operating environments** because they provide a **graphical user interface** (**GUI**, pronounced "goo-ey") that acts as a liaison between the user and all of the computer's hardware and software. In addition to the operating system, Windows and the Mac OS also include utilities, device drivers, and some application programs that perform common tasks.

Utilities are another category of system software that augment the operating system by taking over some of its responsibility for allocating hardware resources. There are many utilities that come with the operating system, but some independent software developers offer utilities for sale separately. For example, Norton Utilities is a very popular collection of utility software.

Each peripheral device requires a **device driver**, or simply **driver**, which is system software that helps the computer communicate with that particular device. When you add a device to an existing computer, part of its installation includes adding its device driver to the computer's configuration.

The last type of system software is computer **programming languages**, which a programmer uses to write computer instructions. The instructions are translated into electrical signals that the computer can manipulate and process. Some examples of popular programming languages are BASIC, Visual Basic, C, C++, Ada, Java, JavaScript, CGI, and Perl.

As you get ready to make your recommendations to Mr. Paik, you realize that the primary factor in deciding the computer specifications you choose to purchase is the software his employees will be using.

Application Software

Application software enables you to perform specific computer tasks. In the business world, some examples of tasks that are accomplished with application software are document production, spreadsheet calculations, and database management. In addition, businesses sometimes use graphics and presentation software, including multimedia applications.

Document production software includes word processing software, desktop publishing software, e-mail editors, and Web authoring software. All of these production tools have a variety of features that assist you in writing and formatting documents. Most offer **spell checking** to help you avoid typographical and spelling errors, as shown in Figure 28.

Spell checking a document ◄ **Figure 28**

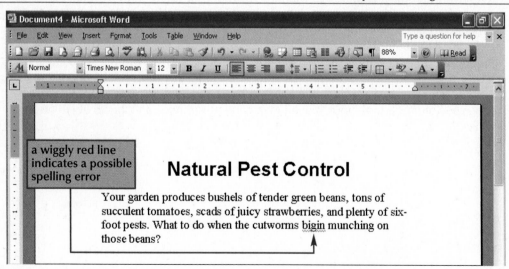

Many also assist you with grammar checking and thesaurus tools to improve your writing by offering suggestions and alternatives. Most document production software allows you to perform **copy-and-paste** and **cut-and-paste operations**; these operations allow you to copy or move words around. Document production software may also include **search** or **replace** features that allow you to look for a sequence of characters and substitute new text.

A **document template** is a preformatted document into which you type your text. A template might include format settings such as margins, line spacing, **font** (the style of type), and font size. Templates make it easier to produce consistent documents, such as letterhead or business cards. Figure 29 shows some of the document templates available with Microsoft Word, a popular word processing software package.

| Figure 29 | **Document templates** |

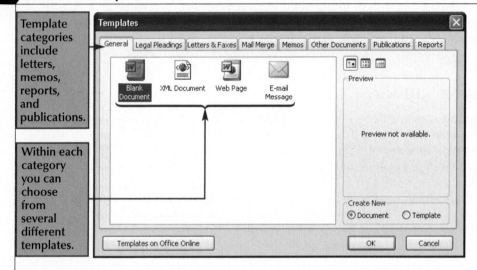

Template categories include letters, memos, reports, and publications.

Within each category you can choose from several different templates.

Desktop publishing software is a variation of word processing software that focuses on the format or printed appearance of documents. It is particularly useful for the design of brochures, posters, newsletters, and other documents that are printed in special sizes and formats. Desktop publishing features, such as automatic page numbering and the use of styles, facilitate the development of multiple-page documents. A **style** is a collection of formatting options that are given a name and used repeatedly throughout a document to maintain consistency. Most word processing software includes desktop publishing features such as the automatic generation of a table of contents or index and the ability to insert graphics.

Data communications makes possible the production of documents referred to as **electronic publishing**. Instead of printing and distributing documents on paper, many businesses and individuals are transmitting them electronically by including them in e-mail messages, posting them to the World Wide Web, or participating in electronic conferences where participants can view documents simultaneously. **Web authoring software** allows you to easily create Web pages. With Web authoring software, you can add text, images, links, animation, and sound to a Web page for a Web site. You can also transform word processing documents into Web pages.

Spreadsheet software is a numerical analysis tool that both businesses and individuals use extensively. You can use spreadsheet software, for example, to maintain your checkbook register. Most people use a calculator to keep track of their bank accounts, but using a spreadsheet has several advantages. Spreadsheet software creates a **worksheet**, composed of a grid of columns and rows. Each column is lettered, and each row is numbered. The intersection of a column and row is a **cell**, and each cell has a unique address, called its **cell reference**. Figure 30 shows a typical worksheet that includes a simple calculation.

A typical worksheet | **Figure 30**

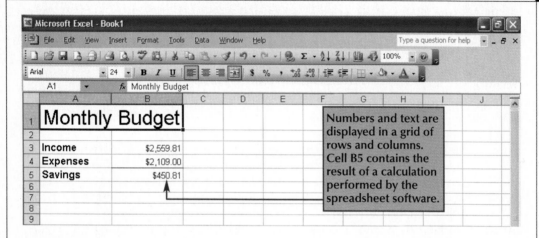

You type numbers into the grid, then create formulas that perform calculations using these numbers. In many ways, a spreadsheet is the ultimate calculator. Once your numbers are on the screen, you don't have to reenter them when you want to redo a calculation with revised or corrected numbers.

With the appropriate data and formulas, you can use an electronic spreadsheet to prepare financial reports, analyze investment portfolios, calculate amortization tables, examine alternative bid proposals, and project income, as well as perform many other tasks involved in making informed business decisions. As an additional benefit, spreadsheet software allows you to produce graphs and reports based upon the data. Figure 31 shows the data in the spreadsheet in Figure 30 represented as a simple graph.

Figure 31 ▸ **Worksheet data displayed as a graph**

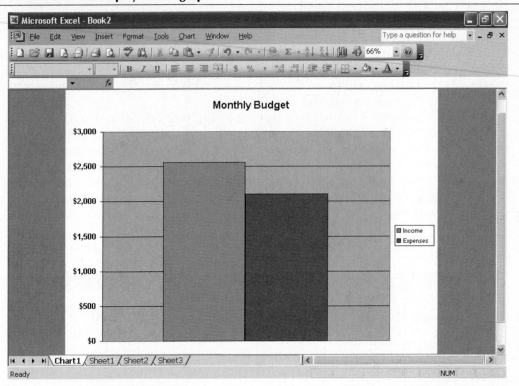

One of the most common types of application software is database management software, which lets you collect and manage data. A database is a collection of information stored on one or more computers. The explosion of information in our society is primarily organized and managed in databases. A structured database is organized in a uniform format of records and fields. A record is a collection of data items in a database. A **field** is one piece of information in the record. Data is the actual information in a field. A familiar example of a structured database is the online catalog of books at a library. This database contains one record for each book in the library, and within each record, several fields that identify the title, the author, and the subjects that the book can be classified under. The information in each field is the data for that record.

Structured databases typically store data that describes a collection of similar entities. Some other examples are student academic records, medical records, a warehouse inventory, or an address book.

A **free-form database** is a loosely structured collection of information, usually stored as documents rather than as records. The collection of word processing documents you have created and stored on your computer is an example of a free-form database. Another example is an encyclopedia stored on a CD-ROM containing documents, photographs, and even video clips. The most familiar example of a free-form database in our society is the World Wide Web with its millions of documents stored worldwide.

Graphics and **presentation software** allow you to create illustrations, diagrams, graphs, and charts that can be projected before a group, printed out for quick reference, or transmitted to remote computers. Most application software allows you to include graphics that you can create yourself using graphics software, such as Microsoft Paint or Adobe PhotoShop. You can also use **clip art**, simple drawings that are included as collections with many software packages. Figure 32 shows a slide from a presentation created in Microsoft PowerPoint—a popular presentation software program that allows you to create colorful presentations and transparencies.

Figure 32 | **Presentation software**

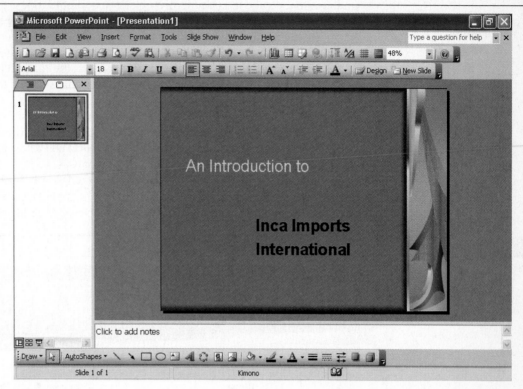

Many programs allow users to use data created in one application in a document created by another application. In fact, it is so easy to add a graphic to your word processing document that you may forget the graphic was created and saved using graphics software. **Object linking and embedding** (**OLE**) refers to the ability to use data from another file, called the **source**. **Embedding** occurs when you copy and paste the source data in the new file. Think of embedding as taking a snapshot of the original. No matter what happens to the original, you still have the copy, as it appeared when you first copied it. **Linking** allows you to create a connection between the source data and the copy in the new file. The link updates the copy every time a change is made to the source data. The seamless nature of OLE among some applications is referred to as **integration**, and the ability to integrate data from all of your applications has become an important skill in business.

Photo editing software allows you to manipulate digital photos. You can make the images brighter, add special effects to the photo, add additional images to a photo, or crop the photo to include only relevant parts of the image. Examples of photo editing software are Adobe Photoshop and Microsoft Picture It!

Multimedia authoring software allows you to record digital sound files, video files, and animations that can be included in presentations and other documents. Macromedia Director and MicroMedium Digital Trainer Professional are two examples of software that you can use to create files that include multimedia. You can sequence and format the screens into tutorials or presentations. Like Web authoring software, multimedia authoring software also uses hypertext to link documents so that the reader can easily navigate from one document to another. Most application software allows users to integrate these multimedia elements into other types of files.

Finally, you must also consider **information management** software. Business people benefit greatly from using this type of software, which keeps track of their schedules, appointments, contacts, and "to-do" lists. Most e-mail software allows users to add all the information about contacts to the list of e-mail addresses. In addition, some software, such as Microsoft Outlook, combines a contact list with information management components, such as a calendar and to-do list. Some information software allows you to synchronize information between a PDA and a desktop or notebook computer. The main screen of Microsoft Outlook is shown in Figure 33.

| Figure 33 | Information management software |

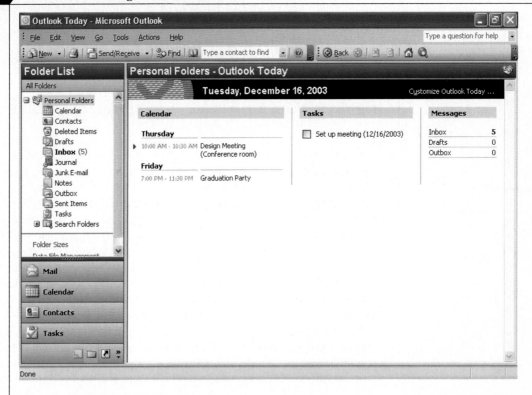

You are now ready to approach Mr. Paik with your recommendations for personal computer hardware, network access, and software. Look back at Figure 1 to be sure that you understand each specification listed. Also consider the software options you should recommend. What will you include? The computer ad already lists Microsoft Windows, so your recommendation should include document production, spreadsheet, and database management software that is compatible with Microsoft Windows. Current versions of Windows include e-mail and network communication software, including Web browsing and Web authoring software. Here's hoping that Mr. Paik approves your recommendations. Good luck!

Review

Tutorial Summary

In this tutorial, you learned about computers and their components. You learned about the different types of computers and their uses. You also learned about peripheral devices and how they are connected to the computer. You learned to distinguish between input and output, and you learned how a computer processes data. You then learned about the motherboard and its components, how a computer stores information, and how information is transmitted. You learned that computers can be connected to form networks and that networks can communicate with each other. Finally, you learned about software and how to distinguish between system and application software.

Key Terms

access time
analog signals
application software
architecture
ASCII (American Standard
    Code for Information
    Interchange)
binary digits (bits).
boot process
booting up
bps
byte
cable
cache
cache memory
card
CD-R
CD-ROM (Compact Disk
    Read Only Memory)
CD-RW
cell
cell reference
central processing unit (CPU)
channel
character-based display
cps
chip
client
client/server network
clip art
clock speed
commands

complementary metal oxide
    semiconductor (CMOS)
computer
computer system
configuration
controller card
copy-and-paste operation
CRT (cathode ray tube)
    monitor
cut-and-paste operation
data
data bus
data communications
data files
database
database management
    software
desktop computer
desktop publishing software
device driver
digital signals
diskette
document production
    software
document template
dot matrix printer
dot pitch
driver
DVD (Digital Video Disk)
e-mail (electronic mail)
electronic publishing
embed
ergonomic

executable file
expansion card
expansion slot
field
file
flat panel monitor
floppy disk
font
free-form database
gateway
gigabyte (GB)
gigahertz (GHz)
graphics software
graphical user interface (GUI)
graphics accelerator card
graphics card
graphics display
hand-held computer
hard copy
hard disk drive
hardware
hyperlink (link)
I/O
information management
    software
ink-jet printer
input
input device
integration
interface card
Internet
Kbps
keyboard

kilobyte (KB)
laptop computer
laser printers
link
liquid crystal display (LCD)
local area network (LAN)
mainframe
magnetic storage devices
megabyte (MB)
megahertz (MHz)
memory
memory capacity
microcomputer
microprocessor
MIDI (musical instrument
    digital interface) card
milliseconds (ms)
modem
monitor
motherboard
mouse
multimedia
multimedia authoring
    software
multitasking
mylar
network
network interface card (NIC)
network software
node
nonvolatile
notebook computer
object linking and embed-
    ding (OLE)
operating environment
operating system
optical storage device
output
output device
pages per minute (ppm)
parallel port

PDA (Personal Digital
    Assistant)
peer-to-peer network
peripheral devices
Personal Computer Memory
    Card International
    Association (PCMCIA)
    device
personal computer
photo editing software
pixel
pointing device
pointer
port
presentation software
processing
processing hardware
processor
programming language
protocols
printer
RAM cache
random access
    memory (RAM)
RDRAM
read-only memory (ROM)
receiver
record
replace
resolution
screen size
SCSI (small computer
    system interface)
SDRAM
search
sender
serial port
server
slot
software
software package

source
specifications
spell checking
spreadsheet software
standalone computer
storage
structured database
style
supercomputers
system software
Tablet PC
tape drive
telecommunications
template
terminal
toner
USB
USB connector
USB port
utilities
video display adapter
video card
virus
virus protection software
virtual memory
volatile
Web authoring software
Web browsing software
    (Web browser)
Web page
Web site
Wi-Fi
wireless local area
    network (WLAN)
wireless pointer
word size
worksheet
workstation
World Wide Web (Web)
write protection

Review Questions

1. What is the key to a computer's versatility?
   - a. software
   - b. hardware
   - c. price
   - d. peripherals

2. Which one of the following would not be considered a personal computer?
   - a. desktop
   - b. notebook
   - c. mainframe
   - d. personal digital assistant

3. Keyboards, monitors, hard disk drives, printers, and motherboards are all examples of which of the following?
   - a. input devices
   - b. output devices
   - c. peripherals
   - d. hardware

4. The selection of components that make up a particular computer system is referred to as the _____.
   - a. configuration
   - b. specification
   - c. protocol
   - d. device driver

5. Moving text, sorting lists, and performing calculations are examples of which of the following?
   - a. input
   - b. output
   - c. processing
   - d. storage

6. What do you call each 1 or 0 used in the representation of computer data?
   - a. a bit
   - b. a byte
   - c. an ASCII
   - d. a pixel

7. What usually represents one character of data?
   - a. a bit
   - b. a byte
   - c. an integer
   - d. a pixel

8. What is a megabyte?
   - a. 10 kilobytes
   - b. about a million bytes
   - c. one-half a gigabyte
   - d. about a million bits

9. Which one of the following microprocessors is fastest?
   - a. 200 MHz
   - b. 2.66 GHz
   - c. 2.4 GHz
   - d. 233 MHz

10. Which of the following temporarily stores data and programs while you are using them?
    - a. ROM
    - b. a floppy disk
    - c. RAM
    - d. a hard disk

11. What do you call a collection of data stored on a disk under a name that you assign it?
    - a. a file
    - b. the operating system
    - c. a protocol
    - d. a pixel

12. Which of the following storage media does not allow you to recycle by writing over old data?
    a. hard disk
    b. floppy disk
    c. CD-ROM
    d. tape

13. A computer display system consists of a monitor and a _____.
    a. parallel port
    b. network card
    c. graphics card
    d. sound card

14. A personal computer that is connected to a network is called a

    _____.

    a. desktop
    b. workstation
    c. terminal
    d. PDA

15. What telecommunications hardware is needed to convert digital signals to analog signals?
    a. mouse
    b. device driver
    c. modem
    d. slot

16. Which one of the following is system software?
    a. Microsoft Excel
    b. Microsoft Windows
    c. Microsoft Paint
    d. Microsoft Word

17. Which of the following is not a function of an operating system?
    a. controls basic input and output
    b. allocates system resources
    c. manages storage space
    d. carries out a specific task for the user

18. Random access memory (RAM) is measured in _____.

19. Disk access time is measured in _____.

20. The clock speed of a microprocessor is measured in _____.

21. _____ is the maximum number of pixels a monitor can display.

22. The transmission of text, numeric, voice, or video data from one computer to another is called _____.

23. A(n) _____ includes a computer, peripheral devices, and software.

24. The capability to send a text message from one user to another user's account where it is stored until the receiver opens it is called _____.

25. The _____ is a huge database of information that is stored on network servers around the world, and which users access by using browser software.

26. For each of the following data items, indicate how many bytes of storage would be required:

Data Item	Number of Bytes
North	
U.S.A.	
General Ledger	

27. Read the following requirements for using Microsoft Office 2003 Professional (taken from the documentation that accompanies the software). Then turn back to the computer advertisement shown in Figure 1 at the beginning of the tutorial and determine if the computer specifications listed in the ad are sufficient to run Office 2003.
    To use Microsoft Office 2003 Professional, you need:
    - PC with a Pentium III or equivalent, 233 MHz or higher processor; Pentium 4 or equivalent recommended
    - 128 MB of RAM plus an additional 8 MB of RAM for each Office application running simultaneously; 256 MB recommended
    - 400 MB of available hard disk space minimum; 880 MB recommended

28. Using the system requirements listed in Question 27, look through a recent computer magazine and find the least expensive computer that will run the Microsoft Office 2003 Professional software. Make a photocopy of the ad showing the specifications, price, and vendor. Write the name of the magazine and the issue date at the top of the photo-copied ad. Write a short paper that supports your selection.

29. You have learned that the use of multimedia requires special hardware and software. Look for current prices and specifications of multimedia hardware in advertisements in magazines or in your local newspaper. What are the highest priced devices, and why are they so expensive? In the following chart, add the specifications and price for the most expensive examples of these devices that you can find. Look at the computer advertisement shown in Figure 1 and determine if the computer specifications listed in the ad are sufficient to run multimedia. If not, write a statement that justifies adding the cost of the higher-quality device you listed here.

Multimedia Device	Specifications	Price
DVD-ROM drive		
Speakers		
Headphones		
Large, high-resolution monitor		

Lab Assignments

The New Perspectives Labs are designed to help you master some of the key concepts and skills presented in this text. The steps for completing the Labs are located on the Course Technology Web site. Log on to the Internet and use your Web browser to go to the Student Online Companion for New Perspectives Office 2003 at **www.course.com/np/office2003**. Click the Lab Assignments link, and then navigate to the assignments for this tutorial.

Reinforce

Using a Mouse

Using a Keyboard

Peripheral Devices

Using Files

The Internet: World Wide Web

User Interfaces

Multimedia